Kindness

MARIA CASTRO

BOOK SERIES BY FIG FACTOR MEDIA

WordPower Book Series

© Copyright 2021, Fig Factor Media, LLC.
All rights reserved.

All rights reserved. No portion of this book may be reproduced by mechanical, photographic or electronic process, nor may it be stored in a retrieval system, transmitted in any form or otherwise be copied for public use or private use without written permission of the copyright owner.

It is sold with the understanding that the publisher and the individual authors are not engaged in the rendering of psychological, legal, accounting or other professional advice. The content and views in each chapter are the sole expression and opinion of its author and not necessarily the views of Fig Factor Media, LLC.

For more information, contact:

Fig Factor Media, LLC | www.figfactormedia.com

Cover Design & Layout by Juan Pablo Ruiz
Printed in the United States of America

ISBN: 978-1-957058-05-4
Library of Congress Control Number: 2021923567

DEDICATION

This book is dedicated to: my mother, Maria Oralia Cuevas-Maltos, the first person to teach me about *KINDNESS*, my husband Martin J. Castro aka Mr. C, one of the kindest people I know, to my sons, Phil & Marty Jr., my daughters-in-law, Jessica & Jessica, my grandchildren, Savannah, MJ, Amaya, Aaliyah, and Adrian, and all my sister friends.

ACKNOWLEDGMENTS

To Jackie aka #Pilotina for allowing me to be a part of yet another one of her divine downloads. To my husband Marty who supports me, my ideas and projects, and loves me unconditionally, my mother Maria Oralia Cuevas-Maltos who is always so proud of each and every project I embark on and tells me so every chance she gets, to my 2 sons Marty Jr. & Phil, who are always cheering me on, my 2 daughters-in-law Jessica & Jessica, my 5 grandchildren Savannah, MJ, Amaya, Aaliyah, and Adrian who I strive to lead by example every day, and for the many wonderful people in my life who day in and day out support me by showing me *KINDNESS*. Most of all, to God for paving the path for me to share this book with all of you.

INTRO

Hello, my name is Maria Castro, and I call myself the CEO of Inspiration. As luck would have it, for this book I was able to choose the word *KINDNESS*, which has such significant meaning to me. This word is something I was taught by my mother as a child.

KINDNESS is free, and anyone and everyone can afford to give it away in abundance every single day. Can you remember a time an act of *KINDNESS* changed your life? We all have experienced those moments, and we all can remember where we were, how old we were, how much it meant to us, how it impacted our day, career, family, or attitude. How is it that some people exude *KINDNESS* without even thinking about it, while others must work hard at it? Can we change the world with *KINDNESS?* You bet. It doesn't take much, and it leaves you with more than you gave. It can turn an ordinary day into an extraordinary day. Don't forget, practice makes perfect! So, make *KINDNESS* part of your daily ritual.

THE POWER OF KINDNESS

The power of KINDNESS can never be wasted or underestimated. Did you know that being kind can help your overall physical well-being? It's true. Have you ever been gifted an act of KINDNESS? How did it make you feel? Did you want to scream from the mountaintop how great you felt? Have you ever gifted someone with a random act of KINDNESS? A smile? A hug? A kiss? A wink? A compliment? Each small act of KINDNESS has the power to transform someone's life. It can even save someone's life. It has brought people to tears, given hope to those feeling hopeless, granted someone the confidence they needed to persevere when they felt defeated. It is like a magic drug that can cure so many ailments that we as humans have.

WHAT'S STOPPING YOU?

If you have never been the type of person to give out acts of KINDNESS, ask yourself: why? What is stopping you? Do you feel you don't have the time or resources to share a little KINDNESS with others?

Why don't you make this your recipe for KINDNESS:
- 2 cups of compliments
- 1 teaspoon of your time
- a dash of positivity,
- a pinch of compassion

Then mix it all together with an abundance of patience, roll it out, place in your heart, and serve immediately!

You can serve up a healthy portion of daily KINDNESS if you follow this recipe. Think of it as a new way of living your life.

KINDNESS IS magic

THE STARFISH

An old man was walking along the beach one morning when he spotted a boy crouched by the water, scooping something from the sand and throwing it into the sea. The boy kept moving down the beach: stopping, scooping, throwing, repeating. *"What are you doing?"* the man asked. *"I'm saving starfish,"* replied the boy, *"If they stay here, they'll dry out and die. I'm putting them back into the ocean."* The old man paused. *"Young man,"* he said, *"on this stretch of beach alone, there must be more than 100 stranded starfish. Around the next corner at least 1000 more. This goes on for miles – I've done this walk for 10 years. It's always the same. There must be millions of stranded starfish! I hate to say it, but you'll never make a difference."* *"Well,"* the boy said, *"I just made a difference to that one".*

QUESTIONS

A million questions blossom when it comes to KINDNESS. How much money does it take to be kind? If you had a million dollars, would you spend it on KINDNESS? Would you share it with those around you? Have you ever captured the look on the face of someone you gifted with a random act of KINDNESS? What do you think the world would look like if everyone practiced a daily act of KINDNESS? What excuses do you have for not being kind to others?

We can all ponder these questions over and over, but truth be told, there is NO reason not to be kind to others. It's free!!

TEACHING & PRACTICING KINDNESS

Allow yourself the time to gift someone with one act of KINDNESS every day—more than that if you want to! Teach your kids and grandkids to practice acts of KINDNESS early on as well. Start practicing and making it a daily habit. Hopefully, it will become second nature to you and your family.

There are hundreds of websites now that you can Google to receive daily updates on KINDNESS. Some of my favorites are Spoonful of Comfort and Coffee Cups and Crayons. Stop what you are doing right now, turn on You Tube, and listen to "Reach Out and Touch Somebody's Hand" by Diana Ross. Wake up to a dose of daily positivity and be ready to become the master of KINDNESS.

Kindness
is a language
which the deaf
can hear and
the blind can see.

FACTOIDS

KINDNESS makes us happier and more satisfied with life.

KINDNESS increases our energy level and confidence.

KINDNESS is good for the heart.

KINDNESS improves our mood.

KINDNESS slows aging.

KINDNESS attracts KINDNESS.

KINDNESS helps reduce effects of stress.

KINDNESS has been shown to increase self-esteem, empathy, and compassion as well as improve our moods. It can decrease blood pressure and cortisol, a stress hormone, which directly impacts stress levels. People who give of themselves also tend to be happier and live longer. If you can be anything in this world, be KIND!!

START A KINDNESS JOURNAL

You can start a KINDNESS journal to see how you feel each time you are gifted an act of KINDNESS or when you gift one to someone else. Keep track of how you feel leading up to it (excited, nervous, happy), how it feels afterward, and how addicting it becomes.

A KINDNESS journal can be just what the doctor ordered. It can help us reflect on times of turmoil that now seem so trivial and remind us of the many blessings we have received. We have the power to use our words to be KIND to ourselves. See how much happier you and those around you begin to feel through KINDNESS. So many times, we forget that we too need to practice being kind to ourselves. In your journal, you can write kind words to yourself: you are beautiful, smart, kind, loving, funny, exciting, and talented.

CHOOSE
kindness

KINDNESS & ADVOCACY

In the late 1980s my twelve-year-old son was diagnosed with Juvenile Diabetes, a disease that I found out affects Hispanics three times more than other races. I worked at a Spanish language radio station and decided to educate the listeners, who, like myself, probably weren't aware of the warning signs or helpful resources. I created a 30-minute segment called "Living with Diabetes" and provided the listeners with professionals who shared their expertise on-air about diabetes and all the treatments and programs available for them. I didn't realize it then, but it was an act of KINDNESS that helped so many people in our community find the resources they needed. Although the show did not run longer than a few months, I believe it made a huge impact in the lives of our listeners who were given the necessary tools to seek proper treatment for themselves or their loved ones.

COUNT YOUR BLESSINGS
(COUNT YOUR KINDNESSES)

Ask yourself to take inventory of the many times you have been gifted with an act of KINDNESS. We all have busy lives. Between work, family, and other obligations, we can all use the excuse that there is not enough time in the day to bother with trying to fit in one more thing. But that one more thing can save your life or someone else's life one day. It can bring you joy and wonder at the marvelous fact that you are alive. If you stop to count the many blessings you receive every day, it could change your life immensely. At the very least, it may change your perspective!

OPENING YOUR PURSE

When I founded **#LovePurse**, a nonprofit organization, it catapulted my happiness thousandfold. **#LovePurse** is putting love on the shoulders of women in need, one purse at a time. We collect and give women in domestic and homeless shelters new purses with all the toiletries they need including a personal note of inspiration letting them know that they matter, are loved and respected. It's not just a purse—it's so much more. The mission is to boost each woman's sense of self-worth and happiness when they open their new purses. This act of KINDNESS has changed the lives of over 1000 women and their families. It has also changed the lives of all the people on the giving end too—a win-win for all! What started as a mustard seed has grown exponentially into something more beautiful than I could have ever imagined.

DON'T WAIT!

If you are waiting for someone to be kind to you first, you may be wasting your time. Take the leap of faith! Gift KINDNESS to someone first without waiting for it to be returned. The saying "tomorrow is promised to none of us" is very true. Why wait? Be kind every single day so that when you leave this earth, you leave knowing you spent every ounce of KINDNESS you had within you. Let that be your legacy. There are times when KINDNESS is exactly what you need to make it through the day. Acting kindly can mean the difference between a good day and a great day!

QUOTES

"KINDNESS is more than deeds. It is an attitude, an expression, a look, a touch. It is anything that lifts another person"
– Plato.

"KINDNESS has a beautiful way of reaching down into a weary heart and making it shine like the rising sun"
– Anonymous

"In a world where you can be anything, be KIND"
– Jesmundo

ABOUT THE AUTHOR

As the Comcast Regional External Affairs Manager since 2005, Maria identifies corporate giving opportunities for core focus areas of youth leadership, volunteerism, digital literacy, and workforce development. Born and raised in Chicago's Pilsen community, her work has brought her back full-circle, allowing her to bring much-needed resources to that community as well as to other incredible Chicago-area nonprofits. She is also the Founder/CEO of Inspiration of #LovePurse, a nonprofit "putting love on the shoulders of women in need, one #LovePurse at a time."

Maria's favorite quote is "if you don't have a seat at the table, bring your own chair and 5 others." She serves on many boards, including the Hispanic Scholarship Fund's Chicago Chapter, Telemundo Chicago's Action Board, and Women's Business Development Center's Advisory Council. She is a co-author of three books and serves as a panelist, moderator, MC, and speaker. She has received numerous awards and acknowledgements including Negocios Now Who's Who Hispanic Chicago, Aurora Regional Hispanic Chamber of Commerce's Hispanic Catalyst Champion, and YWCA Woman of Distinction Award. In 2009 the City of Aurora proclaimed a Maria Castro Day in her honor.

Instagram: maria_castro803
Twitter: @castromaria803
LinkedIn: /in/maria-castro-a843325/
Facebook: /castromaria803
Email: maria@lovepurse.org

www.ingramcontent.com/pod-product-compliance
Lightning Source LLC
Chambersburg PA
CBHW041235240426

43673CB00011B/344